Once Upon A Dream

Imagination Station

Edited By Lynsey Evans

First published in Great Britain in 2024 by:

Young Writers
Remus House
Coltsfoot Drive
Peterborough
PE2 9BF
Telephone: 01733 890066
Website: www.youngwriters.co.uk

All Rights Reserved
Book Design by Ashley Janson
© Copyright Contributors 2024
Softback ISBN 978-1-83565-434-7
Printed and bound in the UK by BookPrintingUK
Website: www.bookprintinguk.com
YB0590O

FOREWORD

Welcome Reader, to a world of dreams.

For Young Writers' latest competition, we asked our writers to dig deep into their imagination and create a poem that paints a picture of what they dream of, whether it's a make-believe world full of wonder or their aspirations for the future.

The result is this collection of fantastic poetic verse that covers a whole host of different topics. Let your mind fly away with the fairies to explore the sweet joy of candy lands, join in with a game of fantasy football, or you may even catch a glimpse of a unicorn or another mythical creature. Beware though, because even dreamland has dark corners, so you may turn a page and walk into a nightmare!

Whereas the majority of our writers chose to stick to a free verse style, others gave themselves the challenge of other techniques such as acrostics and rhyming couplets.

Each piece in this collection shows the writers' dedication and imagination – we truly believe that seeing their work in print gives them a well-deserved boost of pride, and inspires them to keep writing, so we hope to see more of their work in the future!

CONTENTS

Dunbeath Primary School, Dunbeath

Mathew Hampton (9)	1
Molly MacAuslan (11)	2
Fred Thurling (11)	4
Riley Sutherland (9)	5
Mia Mcintosh (10)	6
Scott Norris (9)	7
Georgie Mackay (8)	8
Amber Macleod (10)	9
Eve Simmonds (9)	10
Jacob Mackay (9)	11

Kirkshaws Primary School, Coatbridge

Olivia Ross (10)	12
Sachin Kunderan (11)	13
Ben McConnell (10)	14
Riley Ritchie (10)	15
Kayleigh Angela Cunningham (11)	16
Katelyn Ballantyne (11)	17
Isla Higgins (9)	18
Kade Wilson (8)	19
Euan McCluskey (9)	20
Linken Campbell-Lang (9)	21
Harley McManus (10)	22
Austin Ford (10)	23
Benny Mallon (10)	24
Andrew Collin (12)	25
Logan Toal (9)	26
Hailie Boyd (10)	27
Imogen Colvan (11)	28
Lacey Denny (9)	29
Reece Richardson (9)	30
Ruby Grant (10)	31
Caitlin Collin (10)	32

Murrayfield Primary School, Blackburn

Tom Johnston (8)	33
Kacper Kosztowniak (8)	34
Filip Scharnowski (8)	35
Aubrey Lees (8)	36
Lily Gera (8)	37
Aria Rose Lees (8)	38
Lemitel Ehich (8)	39
Dominik Podsiadlo (8)	40
David Borcuch (9)	41

St Joseph's Catholic Primary School, Pudsey

Ida Taylor (10)	42
Emilie Cooper (8)	44
Holly Millar (10)	45
Cara Millar (10)	46
Emily McDonald (10)	47
Thom Evans (11)	48
Sienna Shaw (10)	49
Harry Borczyk (7)	50
Wiktor Gabrys (10)	51
Jake Dransfield (7)	52
Daisy Lewis (10)	53
Sophia Smith (9)	54
Adam Zamojski (11)	55
Henry Panther (7)	56
Sophia Bartkow (9)	57
Daisy Gartland (9)	58
Annabelle Budd (7)	59

Emily Budd (9)	60
Orla O'Sheeran (8)	61
Sophie Epstein (10)	62
Amélie Gallagher (8)	63
Alex Hayes (9)	64
Joseph Linthead (10)	65
Millie Smith (10)	66
Ellie Harrold (8)	67
Alanya-Rae Morrice (7)	68
Ava-Rose Morrice (7)	69
Olivia Goodliffe (9)	70
Amelia Dockerty (8)	71
Eleanor Braham (9)	72
Jack Blaymire (7)	73

St Mary's Primary School, Banbridge

Alexandra Molloy (9)	74
Clara Cosgrave (9)	75
Adam Norney (9)	76
Izzy Magill (8)	77
Aoife Doran (9)	78
Lexie Trainor (8)	79
Seàn Byrne (9)	80
Méabh Downey (9)	81
Clodagh Connolly (9)	82
Thomas McConville (9)	83

Warcop CE Primary School, Warcop

Abigail Rose Boocock (7)	84
Leo Spooner (7)	85
Emmeline Harrison (8)	86
Faaris Shihadah (9)	87
Riley Lofthouse (7)	88
Luke Schug (8)	89
Harriet Patterson (8)	90
Joshua Batty (8)	91
Lucas Sale (7)	92
Ivo C-D (8)	93

Water Orton Primary School, Water Orton

Amor Hambleton (9)	94
Emilia Leadbetter (9)	96
Ronnie Greatrex (9)	98
Sophia Weekes (7)	99
Harry Roper (8)	100
Joseph Collins (9)	101
Darcey Barnett (8)	102
Summer Wadley (8)	104
Travis Bate (9)	105
Freddie Foulger (8)	106
Ellijah (8)	107
Frankie Cheshire (8)	108
Skye Kight (8)	109
Alara Jennings (7)	110
Grace Morris (8)	111
Harley Jones (9)	112
Blake Braddish (8)	113
Isabelle Collins (8)	114
Harry Mahon (9)	115
Paige Butler (7)	116
Reggie Lewis (8)	117
Billie Diver (8)	118
Lois Fox (9)	119
Esmae Gallagher (8)	120
Peyton Scrivens (8)	121
Sophia Banton (8)	122
Marnie Nightingale (7)	123
Redford Wilson (8)	124
Iona Smith (8)	125
Jacob Saunders (9)	126
Maddie Lacy (9)	127
Roma Bruton (7)	128
Evie Fryer (9)	129
Henry Brown (8)	130
Sylvie Spencer (9)	131
Marli Price (8)	132
Leo Hinett (7)	133
Harry Jones (7)	134
Nadia Ciemala (9)	135
Harleigh Price (8)	136
Frankie Knight (8)	137

Orla Roselyn Brennan (8)	138
Sophia Anelli (8)	139
Olivia O'Sullivan (9)	140
Theia Nye (7)	141
Layla Mernicks (7)	142
Zach Moules (8)	143
Sadie Williams (8)	144
Harper Turrell (8)	145
Louie Davies (8)	146
Lillie Valentine (9)	147
Theo Somerfield (8)	148
Jack Tuohy (9)	149
Archie Savage (8)	150
Jaxson Coombes (8)	151
Zachary Daniel Johnson (8)	152

THE POEMS

Once Upon A Dream

I heard the Hampden roar
It made me want more
Brazil had a patchy team
This could only happen in a dream
I stepped onto the football pitch
I was happier than ever
Did I think this would happen? Never!
When Messi scored again
Hampden roared with men
Haaland scored for the third time
The place rattled like a mine
The Brazil fans felt dread
I felt like a thread
When Neymar scored
Again, Hampden roared
I hadn't scored, I was mad
Because I felt bad
I scored a hat-trick
For my friend Patrick
We won 7-0
It felt like a drill.

Mathew Hampton (9)
Dunbeath Primary School, Dunbeath

Nightmare At 3am

I will never forget this horrifying nightmare
Where I saw evil piggies with loads of slimy hair.
People ran outside carelessly, it was my friends and I
We had just scoffed a whole great scrumptious pie.

We sprinted speedily to the trees with a torch so bright
But it was about to get creepy at this time of night.
We clumsily walked through the many towering trees
With roots so knobbly and vast they blocked all breeze.

But suddenly Iona tripped which caused a domino effect
It was a high-class fall and I gave her respect.
There was an eerie silence before a great big *smash*!
I think someone's going to have a big thrash.

I turn around cautiously and to my horror I see
My friends being eaten brutally by a crazy tree!
I'm shaking so hard I can barely run
I don't want to be shot by a nasty gun.

Then I see a slimy, hairy pig.
It's doing a funky Irish jig.
It's really ugly, but kind of adorable,
With stinky slime so wet, it must be pourable.

He sees me and then grabs my leg.
Then, sleepily, throws me like a laundry peg.
I soar through the air, high in the sky.
I sincerely hope I don't crash and die.

My face is searing and very sore.
But then I finally wake up once more.
I open my eyes, I can clearly see,
A stinky foot as big as can be.

But when I see it, I can find no anger,
For it belongs to one of my best friends, Amber.

Molly MacAuslan (11)
Dunbeath Primary School, Dunbeath

Once Upon A Dream

I woke up on the desert floor,
It didn't feel hot like before.
Then I saw Andy Day,
And then I knew that I was on the way.
Then I heard some stomps,
Now that is a lot.
In my head I thought it was an earthquake,
But nothing began to shake.
Then I heard a roar above,
Then I was surprised by what I saw.
An Argentinosaurus in my eye,
I felt like I was about to cry.

Fred Thurling (11)
Dunbeath Primary School, Dunbeath

Once Upon A Dream

I stepped onto the football pitch and I felt happier than ever
You should see Ronaldo play because he is so clever
There's lots of people in the park
Haaland is coming in the dark
Into the stadium, Messi goes
It is covered in goals
Messi is so cool
Because he has a ginormous pool
They lose the game, it is so cruel
Because Ronaldo is such a fool.

Riley Sutherland (9)
Dunbeath Primary School, Dunbeath

Once Upon A Dream

I walked to the graveyard, weepy and dark.
Nothing like a play park.
This was last on my list,
As I walked through the mist.
As I walked through the graveyard, I heard a scream.

Then, I realised it was a dream.
I was really relieved!
I did not believe.
It was so sad and scary.
Now, all my friends are gone, like Mary.

Mia Mcintosh (10)
Dunbeath Primary School, Dunbeath

Once Upon A Dream

The mowers were ready to mow cow park.
The liners were ready to mark.

The footballers were ready to play.
They needed to pump the ball like clay.

The park is full of cheer.
The footballers need their gear.

The ball is always moving.
The cows are always mooing.

Scott Norris (9)
Dunbeath Primary School, Dunbeath

Once Upon A Dream

So first Torran and I go,
Into a portal like so.
Then in a jungle with a trail,
Full of big, ginormous snails.
It was starting to get dark,
I thought I heard a big shark.
The next day we ate lots of sweets,
It tasted like a really good treat.

Georgie Mackay (8)
Dunbeath Primary School, Dunbeath

Once Upon A Dream

I walked into a forest, dark and cold.
The shadowy trees were so bold.
I swore I saw an eerie figure in front of me.
The sticks beneath my feet snapped from the trees.
Something was following me, it grabbed me by the arm.
I screamed in alarm.

Amber Macleod (10)
Dunbeath Primary School, Dunbeath

Once Upon A Dream

I stepped into school on a normal day,
Then after I got dropped off at The Bay.

We looked outside the window and it was raining cats,
Hopefully, it wasn't rats.

Tobi came along,
To ask, "What's been going on?"

Eve Simmonds (9)
Dunbeath Primary School, Dunbeath

Once Upon A Dream

When I went on the football pitch,
I saw someone called Mitch.
The fantastic stadium called Camp Nou,
Messi ran through.
The ball in the goal,
He celebrated like a mole.
I scored a hat-trick,
Then I saw Patrick!

Jacob Mackay (9)
Dunbeath Primary School, Dunbeath

The Abandoned Cabin

It was a cold Sunday night
Me and my friends went outside
We saw a dark forest and we went in
It was dark and cold; trees swaying side by side
We started walking and I saw a small cabin
It looked abandoned
It had mould, ivy and broken wood with nails on it
Me and my friends wanted to explore, so we did
The closer we got to the cabin, we started hearing something
It was like a light flickering
We went towards the cabin and went in
It had a wooden door and cobwebs everywhere
And a small candle at the top of the house
We went up the dusty, creaky stairs and the front door
Slammed shut
As soon as we heard it, we ran
We couldn't get out because it was basically glued shut
So we broke a window and ran
Some black figure was chasing us
Then I woke up
Safe in my bed.

Olivia Ross (10)
Kirkshaws Primary School, Coatbridge

WWIII In Dreamland

There is a tale about a world war,
An unexpected time in 2024.
Eight countries align with one another,
The choice to betray or become friends, like brothers.

But this war was like nothing before.

This war was magic, with dragons and wizards,
With grass blades of chocolate and colour-changing lizards.
Instead of bullets, there were Skittles and all kinds of treats,
Instead of bombs, delicious, tasty meats.
Throwable pepperoni that will make you hungry.

These weapons or items won't cast war on any country,
The countries swore allegiance, and now are friends,
And at this point, my poem ends.

Sachin Kunderan (11)
Kirkshaws Primary School, Coatbridge

Flying Cars, Driving Planes

I saw flying cars,
I thought they were from Mars,
If I told a soul, I'd be locked behind bars,
I thought it was from Mars,
They were not from Mars,
The cars were really cool,
If you say otherwise, you're a fool.

The next day, I saw driving planes,
The colour of candy canes,
And people had canes for leg pains,
The planes smelt of drains,
They were not normal planes,
They were locked with chains,
And they were all stained.

Then, me and Jamie saw everyone from afar,
Then they got closer and weren't too far,
And they wanted to spar,
Because we didn't have a car.

Ben McConnell (10)
Kirkshaws Primary School, Coatbridge

Dinosaur Land

Dinosaurs everywhere, left and right,
Some are dark, some are bright.
I want to know where the T-rexes are,
I just hope they're not that far.
I'm going to search the whole desert,
Hoping I'm not eaten for dessert.
I know I will find them today,
I hope they're coming this way.
Now the ground is starting to rumble,
Then I hear a very low grumble.
Over there, they're coming this way,
I don't want to be dinner today.
Here they come, but I'm stuck,
In this disgusting, yucky muck.
I close my eyes and put down my head,
Waking to find I'm safe in my bed.

Riley Ritchie (10)
Kirkshaws Primary School, Coatbridge

Black And White

In my dreams every night,
I always see a weird sight,
Once again, I saw black and white,
Then I saw a bit of light,
Again, it was as bright as starlight,
As I came upon the land, the starlight was shining down,
The creatures jumping out gave me a frown,
I tried to book a flight, but it wasn't quite right,
I was sitting upright, it didn't feel polite,
The creatures were coming closer, it didn't look right,
They were ready to bite, I was ready to bite,
I was ready to fight,
I woke up getting a big fright,
It turned out it was a dream,
I was alright.

Kayleigh Angela Cunningham (11)
Kirkshaws Primary School, Coatbridge

The Pink Arena

In my dreams, I arrived at the yard,
With my friend who thought it was large.
We saw the arena, it was all pink,
Last time I came, it looked like an ice rink.
Then I saw a horse, ready for a show,
When the show started, the horse was very slow.
Then the horse went over a jump,
All of a sudden, I heard a big thump.
I was wondering what the thump was,
It turned out it was just a falling jump.
Then the pink arena changed back to its normal colour,
But I noticed it was just the sunlight as it got duller.
Then I woke up with a smile,
Then I went on a walk for one mile.

Katelyn Ballantyne (11)
Kirkshaws Primary School, Coatbridge

Spooky House

S o dark it's making me feel scared
P lanning how to escape this huge and creepy house
O nly I could stumble upon this creepy house
O dd noises such as the creaking of the old building
K ind of late, it's almost midnight
Y elling now, I hear yelling

H ouse full of dangerous monsters
O nly dark, no lights at all
U nder the ground, I hear footsteps
S o scary; I can feel goosebumps all over my arms
E normous monsters coming to get me.

Isla Higgins (9)
Kirkshaws Primary School, Coatbridge

The Shape-Shifting Boy

One day I saw a shed
And I went into the shed
I saw a monster portal
I woke up in my bed
And I said
I want to be a rapper
I turned into a rapper
And I noticed I could shape-shift
And my name was Kade
I shifted into a dog and played
With a ball
I shifted into a cat
I shifted into a monkey
And did a backflip
And I shifted into The Weeknd and sang
'Save Your Tears For Another Day'.

Kade Wilson (8)
Kirkshaws Primary School, Coatbridge

Jerome Horwitz

J oyful George and Harold
E pic comics
R ated a PG
O dd principal
M ade for kids
E pic movie

H umungous villains
O dd parents
R ight show for kids to watch
W ill you watch it?
I t is the best show tied with Mr Bean
T ake a look at Melvin's Inventions
Z ombies Take Over episode.

Euan McCluskey (9)
Kirkshaws Primary School, Coatbridge

An Epic Quest

Epic quest, King's behest
Brave knight, shining bright
Noble steed, takes the lead
Fading light, darkest night
Underpowered, little coward
Feeling fear, shed a tear
Kingdom of light, reaching sight
Monster shadow, chances narrow
Light is gone, bring the dawn
Battle begun, rising sun
Certain defeat, quest complete
Light restored, greatest reward.

Linken Campbell-Lang (9)
Kirkshaws Primary School, Coatbridge

The Floating Sea

Floating across the sea,
There's nowhere else to be!
If you see a boat,
Please alarm me!
Oh no! There's a pirate,
But not close to me!
Please help, they're coming towards me,
Oh, look, there's a bear,
Quick, paddle towards it there,
Coming quick, I'm going to be sick,
Quick, quick, quick,
I have to think quick,
Oh no!

Harley McManus (10)
Kirkshaws Primary School, Coatbridge

The Dragon

One day, I was in a field,
I found a shiny dragon's lair that was sealed.
I went into the forest to find another way in,
I found a small gap, I was glad I'm very thin.
I saw a dragon's shiny egg,
To take it with me, I hoped I didn't have to beg.
All of a sudden, I heard a thud above my head,
Then I awoke in my comfy bed.

Austin Ford (10)
Kirkshaws Primary School, Coatbridge

A Week In Brightland

I usually have a normal dream
But this one I didn't wake up to a beam
I didn't see anything at first
But when I saw the giant land of grass, I burst!
There was a creature called Tizzle
He was half-donkey, half-lemon drizzle
He gave me a power which let me shoot lasers out my hand
He was so cool, he was in a band.

Benny Mallon (10)
Kirkshaws Primary School, Coatbridge

Pineapple Pizza

Sir can I please have a pizza with pineapple,
Because it's as crunchy as an apple.
And the juice is as runny,
As a big blob of honey.
The crust is as hard,
As a big, strong guard.
It is as tasty,
As an enormous pastry.
And I absolutely love,
Almost as much as a dove.

Andrew Collin (12)
Kirkshaws Primary School, Coatbridge

Football Fans

F ans everywhere
O ld fans
O dd fans
T alented footballers
B rave goalkeepers
A nnoying screams
L ittle kids
L arge kids

F ilthy footballers
A ggressive fans
N ice fans
S cared fans.

Logan Toal (9)
Kirkshaws Primary School, Coatbridge

Scary Monster

I woke up and saw a monster sleeping,
He was snoring, it sounded like beeping.
The monster woke up and roared,
I tried to hit it with a metal board.
He chased us around the PE hall,
So I gave my brother a call.
Tommy scared the monster away,
So to celebrate we went to play.

Hailie Boyd (10)
Kirkshaws Primary School, Coatbridge

Untitled

I am a unicorn, Sparkles is my name
I saw a car pass with a red flame
I hopped in the car as it went past
When I sat down it zoomed really fast
We got out the car
He was looking for a spa
He looked a bit tragic
He then ran away
So I went to play.

Imogen Colvan (11)
Kirkshaws Primary School, Coatbridge

Untitled

3000 years ago, a witch came to town
Her face was wrinkled 'cause of her frown
She had a pointy hat
And she looked quite fat
She had a scary black cat
Her cabin was filled with rats
The cauldron was black and shiny
It made you feel tiny.

Lacey Denny (9)
Kirkshaws Primary School, Coatbridge

Doggy World

D rastic dogs
O dd dogs
G reat dogs
G igantic dogs
Y apping dogs

W onderful dogs
O dd land
R ad doggy house
L and of dogs
D ogs everywhere.

Reece Richardson (9)
Kirkshaws Primary School, Coatbridge

Chocolate Land

I go to sleep and look around
I find myself in a chocolate town
I look around and find a chocolate butterfly
Waving her little wings goodbye
Chocolate is my favourite sweet
When my mum asks if I want some, I put her on repeat.

Ruby Grant (10)
Kirkshaws Primary School, Coatbridge

Skye

S kye loved to watch the fluffy clouds dance
K nowing silent time will be next
Y awning on her favourite pink blanket
E ating a piece of crispy bacon.

Caitlin Collin (10)
Kirkshaws Primary School, Coatbridge

Footballer

F ootballers are the best
O ranges are great
O range juice is the best
T ackles are good
B lue is the colour of the sky
A pples are my second favourite fruit
L asers are dangerous
L ewis is my best friend
E ating is the best
R unning is good for you

Tom Johnston (8)
Murrayfield Primary School, Blackburn

Football

F ootball is a round thing
O n the beach we play football
O n the football pitch I play there
T o be honest I like to play football
B all is a cool thing to kick
A ll I want is new trainers
L ike football and Leo Messi
L ove football, that is true.

Kacper Kosztowniak (8)
Murrayfield Primary School, Blackburn

Football

F ootball, Ronaldo shot twenty goals
O o, I got an ice cream
O o, Ronaldo got a World Cup
T hen I got dinner
B each, I went to the beach
A h, Lala is the best
L OL, I got sweets
L OL, ice cream cost 1p.

Filip Scharnowski (8)
Murrayfield Primary School, Blackburn

Dream

D ancing is my favourite thing to do, even my friends like it.
R eading is also my favourite thing to do.
E ven tig is my favourite thing.
A dancer came up to me dancing.
M y mum shouted at me to come home.

Aubrey Lees (8)
Murrayfield Primary School, Blackburn

Dream

D ave was making a potion
R illey is a unicorn, she's crazy
E lliot is a clown, he knows how to do magic
A mber is a unicorn, she's cute
M at is a wizard, he was making a potion with Dave.

Lily Gera (8)
Murrayfield Primary School, Blackburn

Dream

D avid was a bad footballer
R eally bad at football
E ven Ronaldo said he was bad
A ria said he was not bad because he scored a goal
M ack said he was so bad.

Aria Rose Lees (8)
Murrayfield Primary School, Blackburn

Dream

D ream where
R unning in the field, he
E ats a hot dog, he saw
A bear in the field, he
M elted in the field and the bear went *boom*.

Lemitel Ehich (8)
Murrayfield Primary School, Blackburn

Untitled

D inosaurs
R oar
E ric plays games.
A dinosaur chased my family!
M y mum chased my dinosaur and me.

Dominik Podsiadlo (8)
Murrayfield Primary School, Blackburn

Untitled

D ad plays football
R ound and round we run
E at food
A pples at home time
M essi plays football.

David Borcuch (9)
Murrayfield Primary School, Blackburn

The Rainbow Of My Dreams

Red is for the creepy dreams
They make me scream and stomp
They may be filled with laser beams
Or monsters in a swamp.

Orange is for the funny dreams
They sometimes make me laugh
They're like weird or crazy memes
With a short and stubby giraffe.

Yellow is the happy one
It makes me want to jump
I run around and have some fun
Then fall down with a thump.

Green is for a peaceful dream
That lets me settle down
I can picture any theme
And they do not make me frown.

Blue is for the sad times
Swirling in my head
Mountains I can't climb
My mind is full of dread.

And finally, it's purple
The most worrying colour around
It's hard to keep life simple
If something's lost not found.

That's the end of my rainbow
That comes to me every night
A colourful, bright combo
That helps me to cuddle up tight.

Ida Taylor (10)
St Joseph's Catholic Primary School, Pudsey

Always Have Fun In The Park

Today is a good day,
We get to go to the park to play.
We are so giddy when we get out of the car.
We head straight to the monkey bar.
This is a little bit tricky for me,
So I look around,
"Oh look what I can see!"

I see people having fun and others going to run,
To see where they can find, a place to hide.
"Oh wow, I can hide under that slide," said a girl.

I run for the swings, they go so high.
I'm as high as the sky, I feel like I can fly.

There is a dog in the park,
It is cute but annoying when it barks.

Across the park I see the man
Who sells the best ice cream from his van.
A little boy bought a lolly,
But then dropped it on the floor, what a wally!

When I have eaten all my yummy ice cream from the cone,
My mummy says it is time to go home.

Emilie Cooper (8)
St Joseph's Catholic Primary School, Pudsey

The Writer

I dreamt I was a writer of adventure stories
And had a sausage dog called Fury.
I was writing a book in my little nook
When I had an idea that I should go for a beer
With my favourite author and illustrator.
I picked up a book I had written
And took it with me to see them and their kitten.
I wanted to show them my new novel
About treehouses, forests and a runaway penguin
But I got in my car and it had a broken engine
So I ran all the way there while I waited for repair.
They told me they would publish my book
And I was over the moon
That with one look it would be done so soon.
I thought I was going to help them write their books
And eat marshmallows and not have to cook
But my alarm clock went off
And I got up for school feeling cool.

Holly Millar (10)
St Joseph's Catholic Primary School, Pudsey

Sweets, Glorious Sweets!

I woke up this morning in a place unknown,
I was with my friends, at least not alone.
Chocolate fountains pouring down,
Skittle trees scattered all around.

Pinball mountains high and low,
Eat a gumball blow, blow, blow.
But what we saw next was a horrible sight,
A marshmallow monster gave us a fright.

Ten feet tall, was the monster's size,
So we ate some sweets and started to rise.
I was named Pinball Wonder and I was ready to fight,
My friends were called Magnificent Marshmallow and Fantastic Flight.

We tossed and we threw sweets,
Dodging and twisting ready to defeat.
The monster was gone forever,
We were so happy and we worked together,
Although it might have been a dream, it felt like reality.

Cara Millar (10)
St Joseph's Catholic Primary School, Pudsey

When I Dream

Every night I lie in bed
And wonderful dreams fill my head.
Off to Dreamland, I shall go,
My bed is a boat rocking to and fro.
Such a magical world in a magical place,
A joyful smile spreads across my face.
Playing on beaches and flying too,
There are lots and lots of fun things I can do.
I love this world, it's so cheery and bright,
I wonder what things are in store for me tonight.
I can never wait to have fun and play,
This world is the complete opposite of grey.
I know it is almost time to leave
And get ready for the next day I believe.
My parents wake me up and switch on the light,
But I secretly can't wait for the next night.

Emily McDonald (10)
St Joseph's Catholic Primary School, Pudsey

The Shadowgoth

My eyes gently close
And my bedroom walls melt away
Crooked trees surround me
Shadowing my path and way
As gloomy skies loom over
Fog reaches for the ground
I look around the eerie woods
And hear a spooky sound
Then I see a hideous creature
His eyes two pools of fire
"Should I trust him
Or is he a liar?"
Stepping towards me he says,
His voice like a broken fiddle,
Something that chills my blood,
And speaks a wicked riddle,
"They who go in, never come out,
Nobody screams without giving a shout,
Muscular arms and a sinister glower,
A vicious beast as tall as a tower;
The Shadowgoth is coming..."

Thom Evans (11)
St Joseph's Catholic Primary School, Pudsey

The Sea Dragon

I'm with my brother,
In a different world.
Why did it have to be this? Could it not be another?
Percy stops me in mid-twirl.

It gives a ferocious glare.
Then, I realise I'm breathing in the water.
Back to the dragon, it doesn't give me a scare.

I swim up to it and I smile,
I put my hand up before Percy gets me.
My legs are aching from swimming a mile,
Then I've got the key.

All I do is give the dragon a hug,
Then, we're best friends forever.
Now, I don't think of her as a thug,
Now I know we will not be parted, ever.

Sienna Shaw (10)
St Joseph's Catholic Primary School, Pudsey

Doctor Who

Doctor Who sounds crazy, he is invisible!
Oh no, he is setting up fireworks,
Can't we go stop him or will it be too late?
Tobias says, "We might get there in time!"
But, how do we get there?
"I know," said Tobias. "Right let's build something."
"Look Tobias, I have made a tank.
Also, I have filled it with ghost gear."
"Why did you fill it up with ghost gear?"
"Hey Doctor, we're going to blast you."
"Oh no, don't do it. I will do anything for you."
"Too late now."

Harry Borczyk (7)
St Joseph's Catholic Primary School, Pudsey

An Imaginary Friend

One night I saw something strange,
Was it a person? Was it a creature?
Why was he running near the classical grange?

I jumped on my bed,
Thinking what to do,
Before I went to pull down the curtain's thread.

I told my sister what happened,
She was as shocked as me,
Both of our hearts were pounding
With a fear that the end was near.

Then, someone gave me a helping hand,
Could it have been my imaginary friend?

That's what I thought I'd seen
But as my dad woke me up,
I realised it was just a dream.

Wiktor Gabrys (10)
St Joseph's Catholic Primary School, Pudsey

Dragons

Dragons flying in the sky,
Soaring through the air,
Breathing fire and fighting knights,
Eating countless people and guarding the treasure.
Dragon tamers riding them,
Scales are pulled and used for armour.
Heads are chopped off and used for helmets.
Dragons dominate the world,
Smelly dragon poo makes me sick,
Even if I am one or two metres away from it.
Ouch, I got bitten by it,
I'll die in an hour and my death will be quick.
I won't feel anything,
I could be lucky and find a phoenix
So it could heal me with its tears.

Jake Dransfield (7)
St Joseph's Catholic Primary School, Pudsey

This Dream Before Me

T he sky is starry and bright
H ouses hushed and silenced tonight
I n the air, a draught of wind
S hops and businesses closed

I feel a layer of tranquillity
S ome fairies grab me by the arm

A magic spell coats over this strange land

D istant lands kept the fairies a secret
R inging of church bells is heard
E very fairy's eyes turn black
A nd I realise I am in a dream
M um hands me my breakfast and I am relieved it was a dream.

Daisy Lewis (10)
St Joseph's Catholic Primary School, Pudsey

Memory Collector

In my dreams every night,
I dream of something very bright
Down the nightmare
Up the stairs
Making everything a dream
I saw a memory
Everything was an accessory
It was a flashback of my younger life
Making everything a good dream
And not a scream.

  D reams are good
  R ubbing my eyes as I am drifting off to sleep ready for my dream
  E ntering a world of my imagination
  A magical place full of wishes
  M y worst fear is having a nightmare
  S o until next time goodbye.

Sophia Smith (9)
St Joseph's Catholic Primary School, Pudsey

A Galaxy Of Wonders Far, Far Away

Stars are bright
Eagles have great sight
Uranus is a planet
We indulge in good habits.

And here am I
Whizzing like a fly
In a galaxy of wonders
Where stars are in great numbers.

Unicorns galloping, Darth Vader fighting
Smiles of friends and Avengers uniting
The BFG is running
And Elsa is singing.

Now I run onto a pitch and score top bins
I teleport here, to Berlin
I enter a tomb, where I hear a boom
Suddenly I wake up in a room, full of gloom.

Adam Zamojski (11)
St Joseph's Catholic Primary School, Pudsey

The Winning Goal

I dreamt I was a footballer so lethal and so strong.
I got so cross within myself when I did something wrong.
I was playing in the final, confident I was,
However, I could sense some fans were worried about a loss.
Approaching the end of the game, the score was two all,
I shouted to my teammate, "Pass me the ball!"
I looked up, took aim, and scored and the crowd loudly roared!
When I woke up, I felt a little strange,
Then I said to myself, "Did I just score from long range?"

Henry Panther (7)
St Joseph's Catholic Primary School, Pudsey

Little People

I run through the forest on a lovely day
The sky is blue, the sun is bright
Two blue birds fly and play
I could stay here day and night.

I follow the birds as they fly
And I spot a little town
Where people the size of a pencil dance across the sky
They all have a smile on their face, not a single frown.

I was amazed at what I saw
Something I would never know
I was so excited I hadn't seen them before
As the sky got dark the little people started to glow.

Sophia Bartkow (9)
St Joseph's Catholic Primary School, Pudsey

My Sister

M y little sister Lyla
Y oung and adorable, I love her!

S he makes me smile every day
I enjoy playing with her
S he makes me laugh and giggle
T rampolines are what she likes
E very day she rides her bike
R unning, jumping and spinning are some of her favourite things to do

L yla is such a smiler
Y ou've got to meet her
L yla is my best friend
A nd our friendship will never end.

Daisy Gartland (9)
St Joseph's Catholic Primary School, Pudsey

The Dream Is... Calm And Happy!

C uddling and snuggling with toys
A bedroom to relax in
L ots of things to play with
M y family is always there to cheer me up

A bed full of love
N ice hot drinks and hot food
D oodling in a book

H aving fun in my bed
A hot blackcurrant full of joy
P laying relaxing music
P ets are always there to keep me company
Y ou can do these things to make you calm and happy!

Annabelle Budd (7)
St Joseph's Catholic Primary School, Pudsey

My Dream Future

M oving to Scotland
Y early holidays in the summer sun

D ancing and singing
R espectful of other people's rights
E ducating myself
A n Irish dancer
M arried

F eeling healthy
U nderstanding different languages
T eaching others about God's love for all
U nder two pets (a hamster or a fish)
R eaching out and adopting
E veryone is happy!

Emily Budd (9)
St Joseph's Catholic Primary School, Pudsey

Dream Land

My dreams are wishes that I make at night,
Riding on unicorns, as they take flight.
Playing with fairies, dancing with gnomes,
Swimming with mermaids in their undersea homes,
Sliding down rainbows, swinging from stars,
Jumping on clouds, reaching for Mars,
Searching for pixies and hiding from trolls,
Spying on dragons from hideaway holes,
Eating ice cream and candyfloss cake,
Beep, beep! What's that noise?
Oh, I'm awake!

Orla O'Sheeran (8)
St Joseph's Catholic Primary School, Pudsey

Unicorn Dream

The castle is very lovely,
The weather is very sunny,
Unicorns are playing very happily,
While spending time with their family.

One unicorn finds an alicorn,
Whose name is Sweetcorn,
The unicorn takes it to the castle,
Even though it is a hassle.

They take really good care,
The alicorn is very rare.
Sweetcorn likes her new home
And she often calls it dome.

Sophie Epstein (10)
St Joseph's Catholic Primary School, Pudsey

Wild Wonders

W hen I close my eyes
 I dream of bright colours,
 L ost in the jungle where I
 D iscovered magical animal friends.

W ith my animal powers
 O n a journey, we go,
 N ew humans come to hunt.
 D ive into a new world,
 E scape the hunters,
 R un with a jaguar and parrot,
 S lumbering... at the end of the day.

Amélie Gallagher (8)
St Joseph's Catholic Primary School, Pudsey

Imagination

I magination takes you anywhere,
M akes dreams come true.
A nything is possible with imagination!
G o to a world of your own.
I magine anything,
N ever give up on dreams.
A nyone can come,
T ake yourself anywhere.
I nvite dreams.
O vertake fears!
N othing is impossible.

Alex Hayes (9)
St Joseph's Catholic Primary School, Pudsey

Magic

Magic is flying through the sky
Past Hogwarts, where I see a magical key.
Harry Potter has some water
But then I see Hagrid in a corner.
Then I fly across a bridge,
Where I see a bird on a ledge.
Then I come across the clear sea
And I can see a bee.
It was at that moment I woke up,
Thinking to myself,
What a magical dream.

Joseph Linthead (10)
St Joseph's Catholic Primary School, Pudsey

I Dreamed A Dream

I dreamed a dream,
Full of magic and wonder,
With fairies and dragons,
And lightning and thunder.

Pirates and princesses,
All sorts of monsters and ghouls,
Aliens and astronauts,
And yet, all kinds of fools.

I made friends with a dancer,
But with a clown, I didn't try,
Happy yet sad,
As I waved goodbye.

Millie Smith (10)
St Joseph's Catholic Primary School, Pudsey

Famous And Footballer

I wonder, I wonder what life would be
To be a footballer and famous, well let's see
I'm famous on the red carpet, don't know what to do
Stand tall, be brave, hold the team together like glue
Now I'm off to the match, so let's see
If I can score that winner, that shall be.

Ellie Harrold (8)
St Joseph's Catholic Primary School, Pudsey

Chocolate World

Off we fly to a chocolate land
Where there is chocolate everywhere.
Chocolate is oh so sweet
And very tasty to eat.
Let's sail across a chocolate lake
And bite the bum off a chocolate snake.
We love chocolate, yes we do!
We love chocolate, how about you?

Alanya-Rae Morrice (7)
St Joseph's Catholic Primary School, Pudsey

Cotton Candy

Cotton candy, oh so sweet.
This is my favourite treat to eat.
Off we go to Cotton Candy Land
Where cotton candy trees sit on sugary sand.
We walk through lollipop trees
And across chocolate streams
To a place where all your dreams come filled with cream

Ava-Rose Morrice (7)
St Joseph's Catholic Primary School, Pudsey

Dreams

D iving into a world so deep,
R unning up hills so very steep.
E very night I close my eyes,
A nd I start dreaming, paradise!
M ermaids, unicorns and the sea.
S uddenly, I wake up and I'm just me!

Olivia Goodliffe (9)
St Joseph's Catholic Primary School, Pudsey

Forest Hunter

The forest is dark and scary,
I ran into a bear who was hairy,
I found a green apple that needed a clean,
I gave it a wipe so it would gleam,
I took a bite, it tasted so sweet,
I am so glad I found a tasty treat.

Amelia Dockerty (8)
St Joseph's Catholic Primary School, Pudsey

My Friend

I'll get out of bed
Where I cuddle my ted
Look out the window
And see my friend
She juggles, spins and twirls
She helps me get my glorious curls
Draws you in with her amazing pearls
My friend!

Eleanor Braham (9)
St Joseph's Catholic Primary School, Pudsey

Santa's Coming To My House!

In my dream, I sleep tight.
I have to get up early, fresh and bright.
Sometimes I dream of Santa, coming to my house,
Sprinkling magic fairy dust and presents,
Delight at my house.

Jack Blaymire (7)
St Joseph's Catholic Primary School, Pudsey

Fairy-Tale Land

Let me tell you a story you see,
About my little sister and me,
One day we were in her room,
So I read a book about magic shoes,
I saw a rip in one of the pages,
It sucked us both into cages.

We saw the Queen of Hearts and she didn't look nice,
She looked like she had killed about a hundred mice,
We were scared and we had to get out,
I shook on the bars and I started to shout,
"Help, help," we cried.

Then Goldilocks came and gave us a ride,
"Sleeping Beauty's in there fast asleep."
We poked our heads in and started to creep,
A magical book was on the side table,
I took it and it hit me,
It was all just a dream,
The fairy-tale characters I was lucky to see.

Alexandra Molloy (9)
St Mary's Primary School, Banbridge

Space Waterpark

Here I am playing about
Goofing around there's no doubt
Then one second I fall down
Straight round to the ground
All I can see is colours bright
Not on my own, that is right
When I turn I'm in space
I can't believe there's a race
Between a unicorn and fairies, yes
As long as I've been floating up high
I am not overloading the drifty sky
This place is full of fun
I never want this to be done
Sadly Mum woke me up
Faster than a water drop
Space Waterpark isn't gone
I'm going to be back and have loads of fun!

Clara Cosgrave (9)
St Mary's Primary School, Banbridge

Seaspace Race

Tumbling and turning in seaspace,
A seahorse challenges me to a race!
I put my seaspace suit on just in case!
At the start, the space horse takes first place!

Not for long as I dash ahead!
The seashore is angry as his face turns red,
He starts getting competitive!
This time he has no scraps to give!
Racing is what he breathes and lives!

He reclaims his lead,
He's reaching great speed!
I know I'm going to lose,
So I decide to take a snooze!

I wake up and realise it was a dream,
I drink my cup of milk and cream!

Adam Norney (9)
St Mary's Primary School, Banbridge

Dream Away

I was up high in the starry sky
I was reading a book on the crescent moon
I think I had this dream in June
Suddenly, I fell off it felt like a push
I was going to scream but I told myself to shush

I landed in a mysterious world on a faraway planet
Far away from the sun
The world smelt delicious like a freshly baked bun
Then unicorns appeared, and a rainbow too
I also saw some fairies woo-hoo!

I heard my mum call and I started to pout
I want to have that dream again there's no doubt.

Izzy Magill (8)
St Mary's Primary School, Banbridge

Ice Cream

I n my dreams, I see ice cream,
C ircles of sugar sweetness make me scream,
E xceptional flavours pop into my head, beams of ice cream are waiting ahead,

C ylinders of coldness fill the shelves, while some sit magically for the elves,
R ainbow and rare ones go to the back, while other ones have the craic!
E verlasting mint is on sale,
A fairy magical ice waits in a pail,
M um says, "Wake up sleepy head, why did you take so long to get out of bed?"

Aoife Doran (9)
St Mary's Primary School, Banbridge

Unicorns

I believe unicorns are sparkly,
with sparkly covered manes,
shimmering in the light
and shading over.

I can see them in my dreams,
I go to sleep and suddenly...
a unicorn appears.

I reach out,
I feel its fluffy soft coat.
I open my eyes.
it is magically still there!

My parents call out
Lexie go back to sleep
and it disappears.

I hope it comes back next year!

Lexie Trainor (8)
St Mary's Primary School, Banbridge

The Forest Horrors!

As I opened my eyes I was falling through the air,
As I was paralysed in fear thunder burst my ears,
As the ground grew bigger I saw a vision of the woods,
As I hit the ground I landed in mud!

I entered a mansion seeking warmth,
I heard a moaning! And rattling! And shrieks of horror!
I ran for my life to end up in a corridor,
As the zombies and skeletons closed in on me I screamed!
Just to find it was all just a dream!

Seàn Byrne (9)
St Mary's Primary School, Banbridge

Dreamland

D ainty fairies fluttering around me
R ainbow leprechauns, unbelievable to see
E ight unicorns that make everything tender
A fluffy panda is a car mender
M inibeasts, artists are
L et's start painting a magical star
A mazing strong cats
N ightly doing weights on their mats
D reamland is fading away, luckily tomorrow is a brand-new day.

Méabh Downey (9)
St Mary's Primary School, Banbridge

Out Of This World

In my sleep, I drifted to space.
I opened my eyes wide...
A shimmering ship started to glide.

I looked from my window and saw stars.
Me and my sister had landed on the Planet Glars.

We screamed as a beam of light hit us.
We squeezed each other without a fuss.

I woke up only to see,
I was hugging my teddy, Mr Snuglee.

Clodagh Connolly (9)
St Mary's Primary School, Banbridge

Dragon Land

Dragons flying, Vikings coming.
The Vikings start running in fear!

One of them had sharp gear.
The Vikings came near,
The dragons went for the wagon.

Dragons fighting,
Humans start riding them home.
They see lots of dragon bones,
Over which they will roam.

Thomas McConville (9)
St Mary's Primary School, Banbridge

The Mermaid

A few days ago I rode my horse.
I ended up at a river source.
I thought I saw a mermaid's tail,
But I could not be sure because in front of it was a whale.

My horse reared up.
I did not know I was in luck.
A mermaid appeared above the ocean.
She hit me with a potion.
I dove in after her and realised I could breathe.
That is not something you would usually receive.

Abigail Rose Boocock (7)
Warcop CE Primary School, Warcop

Invasion!

In my dream, I see my hidden fortress.
I spy the door...
I enter my fortress.

A few minutes later, Kai comes in.
We hear a noise, something making a din.

We hide in the vent; I am scared!
The dragon saves the day!

Three years later, he returns
And turns the world into his own, dark image

The Golden Army wins the war!

Leo Spooner (7)
Warcop CE Primary School, Warcop

Last Night I Had A Dream

Last night, I had a dream.
I saw a glitter in the stream.
I blinked and it was still there.
The glitter was everywhere!

I went and had a look.
I did have a little snack,
after I had read a book.

I figured out what it was.
It was an invitation to a competition.
Shall I go, or shall I not?
Will I get tired, or not?

Emmeline Harrison (8)
Warcop CE Primary School, Warcop

Space

Whoosh went the rocket as I zoomed into space.
An army of men sat behind me in disgrace,
You could definitely see it on their face.
I heard a fizz and a whoosh,
And suddenly I was in a rush.
To where? you say...
To save the day!
The aliens were shooting at us in the air,
All of this was actually happening.
Or was it?

Faaris Shihadah (9)
Warcop CE Primary School, Warcop

The Jungle

Walking through the jungle my friends and I were brave
We stumbled across a freaky cave
Inside the cave, we found a snake
Who was very very hungry and we got him some mint choc chip cake
He began to slither
So we ran to the river
We jumped the rock
I lost my sock
Then I opened my eyes
It was sunrise.

Riley Lofthouse (7)
Warcop CE Primary School, Warcop

Once Upon A Dream

One night I was working on the farm
I went to the barn
My favourite tractor was gone
The moon brightly shone
To help me see that the tractor had gone
I went along
Where the tractor had gone.

Luke Schug (8)
Warcop CE Primary School, Warcop

Untitled

Once upon a dream, I was at my farm
My dad was shouting, "Go and get Mum"
I could smell hay and cow poo
I could see the sheep and cows
I went to the house
My mum wasn't there

Harriet Patterson (8)
Warcop CE Primary School, Warcop

The Adventure On The Broom

I was at a castle,
Fires were roaring.
I was flying over people,
Everything looked boring.
I flew to the blue
To find something new
On my favourite broom.

Joshua Batty (8)
Warcop CE Primary School, Warcop

The Sunny Bunny

A pot full of honey
Which was really runny!
The sun bunny took it
In a bucket
And shook it.
It went into her mouth
To her tummy!

Lucas Sale (7)
Warcop CE Primary School, Warcop

Billionaire Boy

I made movies
I made screens
Now, it's just too much for me
That's why I have so much money.

Ivo C-D (8)
Warcop CE Primary School, Warcop

My Nightmare Of My Brother's Deadly Feet

You will dread being near him when his socks are thin,
Because when the shoes come sliding off,
All you can smell is the rotten egg stench.
You may think your toes smell bad,
But when you go near these,
Everywhere you go starts to smell like blue cheese!

The fierce feet will, no doubt,
Make you smell like rotten meat.
One sniff and you could lose your sent!
With one blink, I started to stink.
One day, I wondered why there was a big *thud!*
Turned out, he was bathing his toes in mud!

Even though he can be smelly,
Especially when it comes to those wicked toes,
I will always love him.
Thank you, my brother, Mr Cheesy Feet!

Yesterday morning, I went downstairs
Only to find his toe hairs.
Unfortunately, that night he had been shaving them
From top to bottom!
Now, my story has come to an end.
I just want to say,
Don't go near those toes!

Amor Hambleton (9)
Water Orton Primary School, Water Orton

Flying In The Sky

Imagine flying in the dark sky
Jumping on the moon
You can touch the moon with your bare hands
Imagine touching the moon
While eating the cotton candy clouds
With a grey spoon.

Imagine picking up the different-sized stars
It would be amazing
Imagine putting them in a jar
Imagine looking at the different coloured animals
Running and playing tag.

I bounced back and forth from the moon and the sun
The sun was as yellow as a lemon
There was a baboon below me
Climbing on a broken branch from a tree
I saw a big cloud far away as I looked down
And I heard a loud sound when it started
It was so loud I jumped back on the moon.

When I touched the fluffy cloud I went to sleep
It was as fluffy as a white pillow
And I looked and I saw a willow tree
It was so windy that it nearly fell down on a busy road!

Emilia Leadbetter (9)
Water Orton Primary School, Water Orton

Football Frenzy

The thought of standing on the smooth green grass
Everybody cheering for you
And sometimes the fans are thrilled with your skill
And you have a great match
Or sometimes you have a rubbish match
And you need to check if you have got your boots on.

And if you're lucky enough to make it pro
You can get a house with no mouse
And pages of wages too
And when you get even better
You can get a Porsche with a torch too.

And when you're on the field never be afraid
Think you're the best one out there
And that will never change
Tackle like a lion, run like a cheetah
Shoot like a rhino with a curly tail
Never stop believing
Chase after your dreams
Everybody's waiting for you like a beaming team.

Ronnie Greatrex (9)
Water Orton Primary School, Water Orton

Midnight Walk

When I was getting ready for a walk
I saw an owl and it flew to my window
It had glowing eyes and ants were crawling on the owl
I couldn't go on a walk because the ants and the owl would follow me
So I talked it through but I needed to have a walk
Because I needed some fresh air
Because it was boiling, my eyes might get swollen and really red
So I was walking on a walk but the owl kept on following me
So I just followed the owl instead so he could stop
But the owl kept on following me until I fell asleep in the streets
I woke up two days later but it all was a dream
So I didn't need to wake up because it was all just a horrible dream
So I had some food and it made me feel horrible
Because I am dairy-free, it puts me in a mood.

Sophia Weekes (7)
Water Orton Primary School, Water Orton

Being A Pilot

The engine roars like an angry tiger
I feel proud flying through a cloud
As I get off the plane the wind whistles
Like the teacher blowing it on the school playground
As I go high in the sky
It feels like I'm on a fun, exciting roller coaster up in the sky
The clouds dance and make funny shapes
The crystal-clear clouds are cold
The engines are very loud, but I still feel proud
The plane zooms high in the sky
The controls
There are loads of them,
All I can hear is *click, click, click,*
From the controls.
It's like playing tag,
With the clouds in the air,
But fly in the air instead of on the ground.
Being a pilot is fun,
As the plane climbs up into the frosty sky.

Harry Roper (8)
Water Orton Primary School, Water Orton

Monkey Tag

Monkey tag, they climb and swing
Bananas everywhere, they fly and fling
The river all calm and peaceful flows
As the monkeys have fun, the wind blows

Monkeys swing free and climb
When they see bananas they dine
Screeching and screaming, tossing and shouting
They play hide-and-seek so they start counting

Monkeys run through the forest
They jump for a while running and joking
They cheer cutely but soon they tire so rest
Holding until they find the place to do their pooping

Monkey Lord, all hail the mighty king
Their fur looks so sweet like the wind
Here comes Lord Monkey, the mightiest of them all
Don't make eye contact, you might fall.

Joseph Collins (9)
Water Orton Primary School, Water Orton

My Dreamland Of Marshmallows

Where am I, I am not at home,
I shouldn't moan or groan,
I'm not alone,
There's a fairy on a phone,
I am not alone, not alone.

As I dip my toe into the lake,
It is like hot chocolate and cake,
As I eat some candyfloss,
It dances in my mouth.

As I bounce on the bouncy castle,
It is like I am flying high into the sky,
The lollipops grow and grow,
Until they are taller than me, whoa whoa!

The Easter Bunny gave me an egg,
Mixed in with, can you guess?
Oh you probably know,
It is marshmallow!

Now my vacation has come to an end,
I am so sad and mad,
But I've still got a memory of a fairy,
And a bit of dairy!

Darcey Barnett (8)
Water Orton Primary School, Water Orton

My Fish Wish

When I was born I came out walking on my hands
And a few years later I was doing cartwheels and handstands
When I turned six I started doing swimming
And when entered swimming comps I was totally winning.

My big big wish wish
Is to swim like a fish
In the huge salty sea
Yes, that is what I want to be.

With the dancing coral reef beneath
Beneath my little tiny swimming feet
I would find that very nice
Unless I get a shark bite.

In the crystal-clear sea
But not if there is any human pee
My mouth tasted the sea salt
And my fins flapped like a lightning bolt
So that's what I call my big wish
Actually, known as my fish wish.

Summer Wadley (8)
Water Orton Primary School, Water Orton

Game Hacks

I was playing a game, not in a rush
I got sucked in and started to blush
Then a voice told me to do all the hacks
So you will not get the lacks

Then I started leaping on the blocks
But as I jumped on them, they went to sleep, then I saw a lady
She told me to type O then Ctrl, then I got a key
I was about to pee my pants

I dashed in a rush
Then I bashed into someone I could not push
There was a boss I needed to crush
I won and I knew I would rush

Then I came up against the strongest boss
I knew he would give not a toss
But I won to my surprise
I thought I wouldn't stay alive

You have been set free.

Travis Bate (9)
Water Orton Primary School, Water Orton

To Be A Footballer

When I walked into the stadium
I would never let that ball go in the goal
I love scoring and booing the fans
The players were shouting and booing
Every single fan was booing our team
It was really upsetting for us
But guess what we still won
And when we won we celebrated in front of them, especially me.

The football was crazy, our fans loved it
The manager was scouting other players
So we could have a rest and that day five months ago
That day I retired
And that's when I got a season ticket
I watched every single match
That's when we were in the Premier League
Top of the the table.

Freddie Foulger (8)
Water Orton Primary School, Water Orton

Morning Snack

I went to the fridge,
And I had a munch on crunchy fudge.
The yummy fudge was stuck in my teeth,
I was munching fudge.
I found some fudge in the bin,
So I picked up some crunchy fudge.
Someone saw fudge
And had a munch on some fudge.
The fudge was having a crunch.

I had some sweets; they were sweet,
We ate some meat, the meat was weak.
The sweets were sweet, like wheat,
The meat was sweet, like some sweets.

The apple was as red as blood,
Like a pen.
The apple was like a red crayon,
Just like a pen,
The apple was like a red pen,
And a red pencil.

Ellijah (8)
Water Orton Primary School, Water Orton

Dream Far

Running down a peaceful, calm and shallow lake,
Soon from the sky comes a delicious cake.
Going to a bakery, to see someone bake,
I walk into a cold fridge with a chocolate Flake.

When I see the night filled with stars and the morning sky,
Soon the night is gone, I say goodbye.
I then continue on with my day and say hi,
When I carry on across the lake there are no stars so I sigh.

Very soon I see ice, I realise I'm finally there
And if I look very close, I can see a polar bear.
Soon I feel such crisp fresh air,
I realise it was just a dream, I am at home ready to share.

Frankie Cheshire (8)
Water Orton Primary School, Water Orton

My Sweets Are Coming To Life

The sweets are coming to life!
The M&M's are messing and blessing
Skittles hiding in the mittens
Sour Strips riding on sour mitts
A gingerbread man running away from the oven
Sour watermelons watering the plants
Gummy bears colourful as the beautiful rainbow outside

Haribo packets running into boxes
Gummy spiders creeping and peeping
Creme Eggs thriving and driving

The chewing gums started bickering
Milk chocolate pouncing and bouncing
Dark chocolate dancing outside
Light chocolate fighting with the other chocolates
Gummy bears sleeping peacefully.

Skye Kight (8)
Water Orton Primary School, Water Orton

Gymnastics Fun

When the toddlers have their hair in a bun
They always have such a lot of fun
But they just want to lie in the hot sun
I teach them to do flips and tricks like an Olympian.

In the room, we have a cape
It helps them to always remember to feel safe
They say it is as safe as home
Which I am glad to hear.

They say it's such a treat
But honestly, it's like a meet-and-greet
Some toddlers scream
On the beam.

When they go home
They play on their phones
They tumble like cheerleaders
I do it with my friends
But just wait until the end.

Alara Jennings (7)
Water Orton Primary School, Water Orton

The Trip To Hogwarts

Me and Harry Potter missed the train
So we came out of the train station
Grabbing our broomsticks, we flew over the
Train as fast as lightning.

Zooming through the trees
Like a bird on a broomstick
The clouds were as fast as cotton candy
At last we arrived before everyone else.

When we got there, we went to our rooms
To get dressed in our robes for dinner
In the Great Hall, we could see what the first year
houses were.

Me and Harry Potter are in Gryffindor
But the bully, Draco, is in Slytherin
He is really mean
Goodbye, hope to see you soon.

Grace Morris (8)
Water Orton Primary School, Water Orton

An Arsenal Fan's Dream

There is Saka running down the wing
There are also Saliba and Gabriel defending
Suárez on the sideline doing his thing
The fans see Declan Rice passing so they start clapping.

Jesus and Martinelli have pace
So they just always get the ball chased.
Kai Havertz in all of his grace
And Saka with skill gets past the defenders.

The fans start to smell a goal,
It's with Saka and how it goes
Into the box for Trossard

And back to Ødegaard who belts it into the net
And the fans scream his name all away
To the away side of the Emirates.

Harley Jones (9)
Water Orton Primary School, Water Orton

The Attack Of The Skibidi Toilets

Late at night, a colourful thing opened in the dark sky
It looked like a vortex, I got so scared
But then the thing disappeared in the moonlight
Then I heard a knock
But it was a lie
I was so confused, I couldn't go back to sleep

Out of the corner of my eye, there was a toilet
But it was miniature
I remembered it was a Skibidi toilet
And they were all over my house
I then remembered I left my laptop open
So I ran downstairs

I soon turned my laptop off and funnily enough
They disappeared and that's how I stopped the Skibidi invasion

Blake Braddish (8)
Water Orton Primary School, Water Orton

Midnight Feast

When I have a feast it makes me feel heat
And it makes me want to eat meat
When I eat too much it makes me want to sleep
And when I sleep it hurts my feet
At midnight I have a feast.

Then at midnight, I have a key
And I also have a bad flea
And I saw a bird with a long beak
When I eat I will sleep.

And when I sleep I dream of a bee
I saw a lady with a key
Then everybody saw a flea
At midnight I had some tea.

Then I was stung by a bee
Then I spotted a gold key
After there was a magic flea
Then I sat on a key.

Isabelle Collins (8)
Water Orton Primary School, Water Orton

Being A Monkey

The tails twisting and turning
in the tall trees.
The monkey eating and beating
with the honeybees.

The monkey tails prancing
while trees are dancing.
I was having lunch,
my friend had brunch.

My monkey friends are trying
to get a bunch to fall.
And when they're done,
they're going into a ball.

I'm climbing, even though
I'm whining.
The old oak trees,
the branches fell off
in the breeze.

I feel like I'm flying
like an eagle,
but I'm actually
on a seagull.

Harry Mahon (9)
Water Orton Primary School, Water Orton

Dancing In My Dream

When I dance in my dream I take flight,
But only when it's dark in a starry night,
In the household bar,
Everybody thinks I'm a star.

I think of when I could do a show,
But then I wonder what I know,
When I go on stage and the lights shine,
All the people are going to be blind.

I am red when people say I'm bold,
When I'm mostly really cold.
My heart is normally red,
By evening in the shed.

When it is night in the dark,
I always hear a sudden bark.
In my deep dream,
I sometimes hear a scream.

Paige Butler (7)
Water Orton Primary School, Water Orton

Footballer

When you join a team, it's tough and quite rough,
But makes you get that boot to shoot,
Then goals will be banging in.
When you do some tricks and flicks,
The crowd goes loud.
As soon as you pass the ball;
It starts to sprint
Across the field.

As your career goes on
You will be a professional,
And then you will be
Zooming down the wing,
And banging the powerful
Shots in the back of the net,
With the ball going as fast as a lightning bolt.
You will be unstoppable,
But first, you need to get those shots banging!

Reggie Lewis (8)
Water Orton Primary School, Water Orton

Black Cat Attack

At night, I was in bed about to go to sleep
But all of a sudden I heard meowing coming from outside
So I got out of bed and ran down the stairs
I hit a can, then rolled and hit the floor

When I went outside I got attacked by millions of black cats
I was so scared that they were going to bite me
So I went back inside but after a while
I went to have another look

I was in shock
There were even more black cats
I thought I was in a dream
But then I saw a gleam of the moon
So I was wrong
It was not a dream, it was real

Billie Diver (8)
Water Orton Primary School, Water Orton

The Beach

The waves shimmer like an emerald, as the pretty stretching waves play all day,
I spot some waves on the way.
As I push the waves I get splashed all day,
Me and the sea play and dance all the way,
As I launch myself in the waves,
I love the beach, I gaze at the waves,
In the cave,
I see some peak waves,
I swim in the sea,
I meet new friends on my way,
I feel the sea tickle my feet,
I kick the sea,
It splashes me, the waves prance and dance,
I see some seaweed all soggy and wet,
I see the floppy fish in the sea.

Lois Fox (9)
Water Orton Primary School, Water Orton

The Flying Polar Bear

I was in my bed so calm, so quiet,
But when I heard footsteps I was in such dread.
I tiptoed down the stairs, I was so scared,
But when I turned the corner I saw a polar bear.
As I turned the corner and he saw me,
I hopped on his back and we went to a magic world.
It felt like ages but soon we had to go.

He dropped me off at my bed and said goodnight.
The next morning I looked at my pillow, it was a funny shape.
I lifted it up and a photo album was there and a teddy.
I will never forget that night when I met a polar bear.

Esmae Gallagher (8)
Water Orton Primary School, Water Orton

Nightmares

Nightmares come in the night
But never in the sunlight
Once you're in bed
There are monsters in your head
Through the window, branches reach out
Until you let out a shout.

You could get swallowed by a shark
And all you can see is the dark
Monster-made madness
But all you can see is sadness
When you are alone
You can hear monsters groan.

Monsters' teeth are as sharp as a grinder
Sharpening to turn you into a Fruit Winder
You could fall into a hole
That is as deep as your soul.

Peyton Scrivens (8)
Water Orton Primary School, Water Orton

The Best Day Ever!

I got out of bed to see my dog,
I really enjoyed it, my dog is so fluffy.
I took my dog on a really fun jog,
I gave my dog a bath;
It made my dog's fur puffy.

After I went to the bar,
It was really fun.
I went to buy a new guitar.
Then I went back home.
I went to play on my phone,
I was having so much fun,
My dog began to moan.

Now the fun was almost over,
But there was one more thing to do,
Play with the new comfy chair.
Now the fun was over,
Before bed I ate a tasty bun.

Sophia Banton (8)
Water Orton Primary School, Water Orton

The Land Of Sweets

In a land of sweets
The swerving lazy trees were as tall as a milk chocolate house.
The roads were made out of Hershey's
And the cars of gingerbread.

The bees buzzing, getting honey
The bunnies hopping over the grass
Butterflies fluttering around
Birds singing and twittering about
And ducks quacking about the pond.

People giving, singing, dancing and prancing
Bringing tasty sweets and treats
And more things to eat
Clouds of cotton candy and
Chocolate flowers to give yourself a treat.

Marnie Nightingale (7)
Water Orton Primary School, Water Orton

The Tiger At School

I was walking to school,
And I was feeling so cool.
I walked into the playground,
And I found a pound.

I saw a tiger in a cage,
The tiger was in a rage.
Whoever put him in the cage was bad,
The tiger must have been sad.

His claws were as sharp as a razor,
His head was as big as a balloon.
His eyes were like the start of a laser,
He liked looking at the moon.

He was sad so I let him out of the cage,
And he was not in a rage.
So I rode him,
And it felt like I had wings.

Redford Wilson (8)
Water Orton Primary School, Water Orton

Fortnite

I was playing Fortnite and then,
When I banged into a bin,
It was as cold as an ice cube,
In the game I was eating fudge,
I saw a judge.

I had a dream that I was playing cricket,
And I hit like a pro-cricketer,
I hit it in a window,
I smashed the window,
It was a rich house.
I had a dream that I could kick a ball like a pro-footballer,
And then I could do a bicycle-kick like Haaland.

I was in a rocket,
And then I zoomed to the moon,
The rocket was going as fast as a cheetah.

Iona Smith (8)
Water Orton Primary School, Water Orton

My Thailand Island

There was a beam of light.
It was very bright.
There was a waterfall.
It was very small.

I was on a floating island,
Above the water of the lake.
The island was in Thailand.
It was like the island was awake.

I jumped off the island edge,
I tried to grip onto the ledge.
The wind blew against my face,
It was like I was in a race.

I swam in the lake,
Like a dolphin with grace.
The waterfall was as slithery as a snake.
My Thailand Island is a magical place.

Jacob Saunders (9)
Water Orton Primary School, Water Orton

My Crazy Unicorn And I!

Me and my unicorn have fun all day
We splash in the pool and bathe in the sun ray
We slide down rainbows, shining rainbows!
My unicorn is truly mine
One day... I have to say
My unicorn went wild
I think my unicorn ate something mild
She's crazy
She's lost her daisy
She's dancing and prancing
She's being a nightmare
Like a wiggling bear
And is that glitter goo
She is eating and chewing and finally is it the end?
Goodnight! Crazy unicorn and I!

Maddie Lacy (9)
Water Orton Primary School, Water Orton

A Forest Dream

In a forest in the night,
all animals come to sight.
In hives, some bees make honey.
On the ground, some little bunnies
look up at the starlit skies.

Wolves howl at the full moon,
knowing that prey will come soon.
Foxes come out of little boxes,
having the time of their lives.

Trees stretch as tall as can be,
for lots of animals need the trees.
Little mice build some little houses.
Goodbye forest friends, see you soon
in the light of the moon!

Roma Bruton (7)
Water Orton Primary School, Water Orton

Scary Fairy

This poem is scary
So don't expect to see a fairy!
A person called Beth
Is scared of death.
She was all alone
So she thought it could be a PJ day.
Oh watch out! There's a ghost next to the windowsill.
She sat still.
And all of a sudden...
She heard a scream of a meme!
But it was the friend.
She heard another scream
And it wasn't her phone.
She felt like she was being chased by a cheetah
And there it was, the black cat.

Evie Fryer (9)
Water Orton Primary School, Water Orton

To Be A Pilot

The plane came alive
It did a nosedive
The plane started to dance
Danced up high and pranced

The plane lost control
The plane saw through a hole
The plane started walking
So then I started talking

The plane started talking
The plane started walking
I took control
The plane started to roll

The plane flew like an eagle
The plane squealed like a seagull
The plane was taxiing to the gate
Now flying is great!

Henry Brown (8)
Water Orton Primary School, Water Orton

Fly Up So High

As I lie in bed,
The calm clouds fill my head,
Floating in the blue sky,
As I watch them fly.

My head is filled with bubbles,
It gets rid of my troubles,
The bees,
Buzz around the trees.

As I stare, I see a flower,
It gives me a sense of power,
As I fly,
Oh so high.

Now I'm awake in bed,
Debating if this was all in my head.
I'm sad this poem wasn't real,
But this is how I feel.

Sylvie Spencer (9)
Water Orton Primary School, Water Orton

The Big World

Around the mountains,
there are fountains,
coming by
with you and I.

My little Buddy,
being funny.
I can't see who,
but it's you!
My little sloth,
you're as harmless as a moth.
Swinging on the wonky bridge,
you're like tonnes of kids.

I won't ever leave you!
We're crazy while going through.
The bridge is rocking on its own,
to not get us harmed.

The Big World!

Marli Price (8)
Water Orton Primary School, Water Orton

A Magical Dream

Violets are red,
Bats can be ultra-fed
Trees stay in the wild
But we never see children
In the wild we see
Colours and we see rabbits,
Birds and ultra violets
And we go on a plane with pilots
Flowers are like beautiful honey
We run as fast as a rocket
An ostrich runs as fast as a rocket
Plus plane trees are alive
So we need to dive
Into the pool
And we dress in wool
So we can drool
It is so good.

Leo Hinett (7)
Water Orton Primary School, Water Orton

Magnificent Creatures

The baby turtle was so tiny
I would make it the number eight
It was walking away
And it walked straight

I looked at it, then I ate some food
It put me in a good mood
Then I saw another creature
Crawling in the woods

The creature was quite big
But I couldn't pet it
Then I realised it was the baby's dad!

I met the big one
And I got a friend
Whoooo-hoooo!

Harry Jones (7)
Water Orton Primary School, Water Orton

The Water Park

The waves were splashing and dashing only when the cave was
Crashing and mashing at night
But in the morning the waves were splashing
And dancing like a bouncy castle
With the scary attractions shimmering and bubbling

The big wall that opened and put massive
And fast shimmering waves letting you jump
Off the ground picking you up as quickly as
Possible sparkling and dancing.

Nadia Ciemala (9)
Water Orton Primary School, Water Orton

Doggy Tails

Charlie, Ollie and Milo
They're the three
They love each other
We can all agree

Charlie likes swimming
Charlie likes food
Too much of anything
Is bad for his mood

Ollie likes walking
And cuddles at night
That's why we hold him
Really tight

Milo likes running
As fast as he can
He is almost
As fast as Superman.

Harleigh Price (8)
Water Orton Primary School, Water Orton

Being In A Good Dream

In a land there was a golden beam,
And there were security guards in my dream,
And it was a happy place.

I felt like I was in Hawaii because they gave me a flower necklace,
It was silver because I was a VIP!
How amazing.

The building was as sunny as a star, it was so beautiful,
And we got a VIP room for candy!
It was so cool.

Frankie Knight (8)
Water Orton Primary School, Water Orton

Panda Land

The trees were blooming bright
Bamboo green as leaves
There were loads of beautiful flowers
When I walked in
I smelt a beautiful smell
Before I walked in I seriously couldn't tell

I saw bamboo blooming bright
Within the night
The bamboo was dancing
And the pandas were prancing
I love this land
The Panda Land.

Orla Roselyn Brennan (8)
Water Orton Primary School, Water Orton

The Cartoon Cat Invasion

Once upon a dream, I woke and saw
Cartoon Cat and his sister
They were staring at me and my stepsisters
Cartoon Cat was running to me
But his sister didn't
When Cartoon Cat came to me
I broke his neck
And then I said to the sister Cartoon Cat
Go to my sister
And she went up the stairs and
Looked at the corner of her eye.

Sophia Anelli (8)
Water Orton Primary School, Water Orton

The Beach

The waves dance up and down and the sand flies around and around
The sound of the wind waving, up and down with people sunbathing
There are shimmering shells and there are crabs, one dabs
I go into the water with the coral reef beneath my feet
Seagulls squawk for food, chasing a man with banana-themed shorts on.

Olivia O'Sullivan (9)
Water Orton Primary School, Water Orton

Midnight Snack

When I see raw meat,
It smells like bleach,
To overeat,
I get sweaty from the heat.

Food:
I dream of pasta bake,
I dream of lemon cake,
Roast chicken on
A Christmas plate.

Sea:
In the sea,
I do lots of wees,
When I see seaweed,
It reminds me of a kiwi.

Theia Nye (7)
Water Orton Primary School, Water Orton

Crazy Class

Oh no, the class has gone crazy
They are standing on the chairs and the table
Looking really lazy and standing on the chairs
The children thought that they ruled the school
But really the teachers ruled
The class was standing on the stairs
The books were stacked
The school was as fun as a clown.

Layla Mernicks (7)
Water Orton Primary School, Water Orton

The Ball

I was dreaming then I saw the ball
The dancer's ball had spikes
The sharpest spike in the world
Everywhere I went, even in the pool
Then Sam and Cam called Leo over to get the ball
Then we did it, we destroyed the ball
We helped and everyone said, "Yes, yes, yes!"

Zach Moules (8)
Water Orton Primary School, Water Orton

Body Parts

Feel my feet it feels like meat
Feel my head it feels like dead
Feel my arm it feels like barn
Feel my leg it feels like beg
Feel my ribs it feels like mist
Feel my hip it feels like kiss
Feel my brain it feels like drain
Feel my hair it feels like bear.

Sadie Williams (8)
Water Orton Primary School, Water Orton

Fire Breath

Deep in a cave, something likes to overeat piles of meat
A dragon with an enormous tail
And wings as big as a sail
His eyes shine like diamonds
And he hates lemonade
But he still has a heart made of gold
He is the best friend to keep you warm from the cold.

Harper Turrell (8)
Water Orton Primary School, Water Orton

The Jungle

I heard lots of animal sounds
And it was a pound
Like a monkey and a slow sloth.
They sniffed around the jungle to find some fruit.

I saw lots of monkeys eating lots of bananas
And popping them open,
Even the daddies do it as well,
Yum, yum.

Louie Davies (8)
Water Orton Primary School, Water Orton

The Storm With Flying Monkeys

There was a big storm controlled by flying monkeys,
One minute everyone was relaxed and lazy,
Then the monkeys made the waves go crazy!
It was burning the sand, making everyone leave,
The sand was going in people's eyes and they could not see!

Lillie Valentine (9)
Water Orton Primary School, Water Orton

When I Dream Of Food

When I go to KFC
I go for a wee.
I ask my mum,
She says, "Play with Tom."
Then my mum
Says, "Play with Ron."

I get really hungry
So I sit on my rug.
When I go and tug
I run into the tub.

Theo Somerfield (8)
Water Orton Primary School, Water Orton

Beware, Watch Out!

The man ran from the scary wolf
When I eat I have smelly feet
In the night I have a fright
When I need a wee I have a KFC
He ran from the scary man
He was scared from his head down to his feet
In the sea was a scary pee.

Jack Tuohy (9)
Water Orton Primary School, Water Orton

Once Upon A Dream

When I am on my phone
And my bone
Comes out and feels like chrome
In my smelly bone.

When I dream of food
It puts me in the mood
To overeat smelly feet
Near me and the beat.

Archie Savage (8)
Water Orton Primary School, Water Orton

Monster

The monster's mouth is as big as a hawk.
The monster's eyes were as small as a mouse.
In the darkness,
The monster is at its best.

Jaxson Coombes (8)
Water Orton Primary School, Water Orton

Untitled

I dream of pasta bake.
I dream of lemon cake.
Juicy it becomes on my chin,
Wasted food in the bin.
All night I toss and turn.

Zachary Daniel Johnson (8)
Water Orton Primary School, Water Orton

YOUNG WRITERS INFORMATION

We hope you have enjoyed reading this book – and that you will continue to in the coming years.

If you're a young writer who enjoys reading and creative writing, or the parent of an enthusiastic poet or story writer, do visit our website **www.youngwriters.co.uk**. Here you will find free competitions, workshops and games, as well as recommended reads, a poetry glossary and our blog.

If you would like to order further copies of this book, or any of our other titles, then please give us a call or visit **www.youngwriters.co.uk**.

Young Writers
Remus House
Coltsfoot Drive
Peterborough
PE2 9BF
(01733) 890066
info@youngwriters.co.uk

YoungWritersUK   **YoungWritersCW**
youngwriterscw   **youngwriterscw**